TRANSCENDING FROM TRAUMA TO TRIUMPH:

Getting Past the Pain to Forgive

Author: Lorraine Thompson

*Copyright© Transcending from Trauma to Triumph –
Getting Past the Pain to Forgive – by Lorraine Thompson
Printed in the United States
First Edition
For more information, contact the author at:
wehavevoices2@gmail.com*

*Library of Congress 1-12809654251
February 2023 ISBN: 979-8-9891993-0-3   Paperback
All Bible references used in this text originate from either
the New King James or American Standard versions.
Published by Chloe Arts and Publishing, LLC
Minneapolis, MN
Editor: Julie Dalgleish
All rights reserved. No portion of this publication may be
reproduced, stored in a retrieval system, or transmitted in
any form by any means electronic, mechanical, without the
publisher's prior written permission.*

Printed and bound in the United States of America

Table of Contents

FOREWORD 6

INTRODUCTION 9

ABOUT THE AUTHOR... 16

CHAPTER I: MY BEGINNING.................................... 18

CHAPTER II: MY WILDERNESS 22

CHAPTER III: MY AWAKENING, MY RECOVERY 44

   The Journey to Resilience 50

   The "Domino" Affect: Revelation of "Why Me?" 54

   Perception and Self-Worth 58

   From Hopeless to Hopeful – Activating my Faith 59

   Understanding Forgiveness 60

   Understanding God's Will 62

   Hope and Healing 63

CHAPTER IV: MY PERSONAL JOURNAL 67

EPILOGUE 118

BIBLIOGRAPHY 120

"It is easier to build strong children than to repair broken men."
Frederick Douglass

FOREWORD

By Rev. Charles A. Houston Jr.

There are thousands of people who decide to write books for various reasons with different motives. Some see writing only as a way of making residual income. Some see writing a book as an opportunity to promote their business or company. Others may write because they were told to do so without an inner desire to sincerely share and help the potential readers of their book. I have known the author of this book for several years now and can vouch for the reason she is writing this book. Lorraine Thompson is a devout woman of God who has always presented herself to me as accountable to feedback and correction, genuine, intentional, and compassionate. Not only will you feel these things, in this her first book, but you will also realize that the things she shares don't come from a desire to be popular. They come from a passion to help other people who have been in her spiritual and emotional shoes. Lorraine is not only presenting a book of facts from external research. She is also testifying of the tremendous healing and wholeness that comes when you have faith in God AND do your own personal self-improvement work and adopt proven self-care techniques.

In this book Lorraine addresses various difficult topics that she has had to approach, endure, and/or overcome in her own life journey. She shares various types of abuse that she has been through and the importance of not accepting that as a way of life. She addresses the stress, depression, and anxiety that family dynamics, religious trauma, and personal guilt and shame often create.

Most of all, you will see how a personal relationship with God along with self-care, and a healthy support network of people resources can allow someone to have the testimony that Lorraine has.

She has been healing and "Transcending from Trauma to Triumph". I believe you will enjoy the documenting of her forgiveness journey and be inspired to begin your own.

INTRODUCTION

I authored this book for anyone who has struggled through the hardships of abuse. Abuse crosses all economic lines, all ethnicities, and all nationalities. You may feel you don't have a voice, just as I did. I realized that during the "Me Too!" movement, which focused on the motion picture industry, other voices were not being heard. The Lord spoke to me clearly about three years ago and let me know the silently abused have a voice that must be heard. I hope that each person that reads this book will see that they have a voice and a purpose. You can overcome through a process of healing with the intent to help and not hurt anyone that might have hurt you. You can still have a wonderful life. I chose the title that I now call the 3 "Ts" to describe what my journey was like. To "Transcend" is to go beyond the range or limits. When you transcend you don't allow your environment or society to limit you. You go beyond the circumstances of trauma. After going beyond the limits of the trauma, you will be triumphant. You can and will reach the level of triumph over your traumas. You triumph over your trials by transcending or "going beyond" the crises. Transcending is making a step, even a small step, to move forward. Transformation begins with you! Never let anyone tell you that you can't!!!

I would like to admonish the religious community to be responsive and not sweep these issues "under the rug." Help those that are affected by not only covering them with prayer and encouragement, but also assist them to seek counseling from qualified professionals. Jesus was our true role model and he ministered through compassion and love. The victims as well as those that impose abuse both need help.

The writing of this book has been very therapeutic. I began writing at the beginning of the COVID-19 pandemic in March 2020. I woke up in the middle of the night, and the words began to flow. It was a very personal communication I never thought I would share. However, as I continued to write, I began to realize this was a gift that God allowed to flow through me, and it wasn't just for me; it is meant to be shared to show that you can transcend from trauma and triumph. Writing provided an outlet for me to share my inner most thoughts without being muted.

The title of this book speaks to my experience of being "muted" by the intimidation of verbal, spiritual, and emotional abuse. This abuse was spiritual (I was told you're a woman; therefore, you don't understand God's word), verbal, and emotional. What happened to me is a result of low self-esteem when you allow others to walk into your life to control and manipulate your development of understanding who you are.

Author Brené Brown said that vulnerability is the most accurate measurement of courage. Vulnerability is a strength. The scripture II Corinthians 12:10 (KJV) states,

"Therefore, I take pleasure in infirmities, in reproaches, in necessities, in persecutions, in distresses for Christ's sake: for when I am weak, then am I strong."

These chapters are the transformation of my life, which will hopefully help someone else recognize the pitfalls of uninformed life decisions. I didn't want this to be another "self-help" book. You are the "self" and when you realize that you don't have to accept how you're treated, you are on your way to get the "help" you need.

My story doesn't end with this book because there are still more chapters in my life. There are more chapters that I will determine with God's help. It won't be written in pain, but in recovery and peace. With God's help, I will continue to heal and understand that he created me in his image. Abuse is a direct insult to God. The late Myles Munroe said: "When your purpose is not known, abuse is inevitable."

Forgiveness is about you; it's about releasing those that hurt you. Forgiveness develops the best version of yourself. When you forgive, you release those who hurt you in the past by not bringing them into your future. You can't win if you don't forgive. When you forgive, it allows you to release the hurt; then, the wounds will heal.

I also want to make sure that although my experiences were devastating, my prayer is that those who impose the hurt be healed and set free as well. The abusers themselves are usually victims of the very thing they impose on others. They need healing too. Forgiveness is the vehicle that brings healing to the hurting. Remember, you must choose healing, and forgiveness is the vehicle that will get you there.

When authoring this book, it allowed me to express my thoughts as well as my experiences. My now adult children are still experiencing some aftermath of the trauma and struggle to find themselves to make sense of those experiences. Parents, your children are witnessing what no one should ever see, the systematic and subtle abuse that forces you to suffer in silence. I said earlier in the chapter that children who witness abuse are in crisis and are destined to repeat the cycle without the opportunity to see healthy role models. By enabling others to abuse you and your children, you are not only hurting yourself, but also allowing it with your silence.

Without intervention through counseling and mentoring of positive role models, children in crisis may become adults in crisis.

You can survive and thrive. Change begins with you. Make the decision that you deserve to live and be happy.

<u>You must know your purpose; no one else has the authority to tell you what that is.</u>

ACKNOWLEDGMENT

I want to thank my publisher, Dr. Joyce Marrie, who has been a very knowledgeable resource for my first experience as an author. Her experience as an author. Her experience and expertise are greatly appreciated.

I also want to thank my very supportive husband, Pastor Derek Thompson, who has encouraged me to push forward and get my book published. It has given me the courage to move forward and share my experiences to hopefully guide others to a life free from the pain of abuse.

I want to acknowledge my children, who have grown through the storm and who continue to overcome and recover from the past. You are my precious gifts and I love you with all my heart.

I dedicate this book in memory of my dear parents, Archie and Fannie Starks (Isabell) who without them, I would not be the woman I have grown to be! I love and miss them every day!

Special thanks to my spiritual mother and advisor, Mrs. Dolly D. Foster who has been a source of inspiration and support throughout the years.

Special thanks to Lyresa McGriff for your excellent expertise in trauma counseling, Embrace Counseling and Consulting, Hiram, GA

I also want to acknowledge and thank my church families to which I attribute my growth and support:

    Word of Faith Family Worship Cathedral, Austell, GA
        Senior Pastor: Bishop Dale C. Bronner
    Enon Chapel Baptist Church, Philadelphia, PA
        Senior Pastor: Derek N. Thompson

ABOUT THE AUTHOR

Lorraine Thompson is a native of St. Paul, Minnesota. Her parents migrated from Memphis, TN. She is the 2nd oldest of 6 children. She wasn't active in sports, so she followed her passion of music and learned several instruments, including the violin. After high school graduation, she attended college in the South. She always wanted to experience life in a southern state and thought college was the best way to do that. After she received her BA in Political Science, she went on to receive a MA in Public Administration. She married after college and had a Family of five sons (including one bonus son) and one daughter. When the marriage ended, she relocated to the Atlanta, GA area and resided there for over 17 years.

She then relocated to the northeast where she currently resides.

"If you want to know your purpose, ask the manufacturer."

In other words, ask God. If you don't know your purpose, abuse is inevitable." Myles Monroe

CHAPTER I: MY BEGINNING

I was born in the cold tundra of the Midwest. The Black community was segregated, but we were a close-knit community.

I always had hope for a happy life with everything that I needed. I grew up in a two-parent household; although poor, we never complained. Both my parents were hard workers, although my mom was at home with us for most of our childhood. My dad worked long hours and never missed a day. At one point, he worked two jobs to make ends meet. I remember my mom taking on what they called "day work," or housework, in the wealthy communities. She also worked part-time in her older sister's beauty shop as a beautician.

I had four brothers and one sister; we wore clothing from the thrift stores or hand-me-downs from family and friends. I remember being teased relentlessly for wearing clothes that didn't match. Although my early memories are growing up poor, I always had hope for a better life.

One distinct memory I have is I hated my birth name. Your name isn't just a label; it's how others see you. I always thought that my birth name didn't fit me. One day out of curiosity, I looked up the meaning and was pleasantly surprised that it means "beautiful." I poetically confessed to myself, "You see, I am what I see; no labels are holding me." Although I'm legally using my middle name, it felt good to know that my name meant something very positive.

I grew up in the church, starting at my grandfather's church, then my uncle's. That was my life. My parents kept us in church not only on Sundays but several days a week I had a desire to be "saved" at the tender age of 12. I didn't understand fully what that meant; I just knew what my parents taught me. As I grew older, I began to understand what a relationship with the Lord really is; I realized there was more that I needed to grow and mature spiritually.

Graduating from high school for me was an exciting time. I could finally move on to "grown-up" things: getting a job, saving for college, and finally getting away to start my life.

Although I grew up in the north, I always had a longing to move down south and decided going to college was the best way to experience living on my own and learning a different part of the country. I was always fascinated with the South, although I knew my parents and grandparents had a much different view. I wanted to experience it, and I'm glad I did.

I decided that for my first year, I would attend a Christian-based school in the deep South. I was very shy but enjoyed meeting new people and getting used to campus life. I have wonderful memories of my experience and have gained life-long friends. This was the turning point in my life. After my freshman year, I transferred to another University to begin my sophomore year. I didn't know that I would have an unexpected turn of events that would change my life forever.

CHAPTER II: MY WILDERNESS

I realized that when you're young, you're full of hope. However, your inexperience and naivety does not equip you to deal with being blindsided by unexpected hurdles. I realized later those unexpected hurdles were abuse that was so subtle that it was like a "mind-control" mechanism that completely paralyzed my will, my decisions, and my thoughts. Although the events were devastating, I later realized that this chapter of my life was a "blessing" in disguise. Because my pain would contribute to the blessings for others, and my pain would also propel me to my purpose. This life decision was a marriage that I wasn't ready for, nor was I prepared for the pain that was imposed on my life. This book is the tapestry of those experiences. It wasn't written only to express pain, but to share recovery and restoration. With God's help, I will continue to heal and understand that HE created me in his image. I didn't need anybody to monopolize my time, manipulate my mind, or control my movement.

It was my belief that God created women to be designed to care for the family and not to be the sole provider and overseer in the home within the covenant of marriage. I always felt like I didn't have a covering when I was married because of the tremendous amount of responsibility I had to take care of regarding the financial needs of my family. My husband didn't understand that forcing me to take on more responsibilities than I was equipped for hurt me and our children because I couldn't function fully as the mother of the home. I didn't think I had a voice or a choice.

I believed that I had to accept my situation and not make waves. I didn't have a right to fight about my plight. I cried to the Lord for help, not one plea I could utter to anyone for fear that my situation would get worse.

It was a result of this experience, that I asked the Lord to "order my steps" to keep toxic people away during my period of recovery and restoration. What I did realize is I didn't even know that what I went through was domestic abuse; once I realized it, I understood the gravity of the situation. Abuse is a direct insult to God. I am one of God's daughters, his creation that was "wonderfully and fearfully made" in his image. Being thankful has continued to provide me with newly found happiness by turning my past painful experiences into my powerful purpose.

There were several situations that tragically altered my life. On the evening of February 27, 2001, I received a call from my only daughter revealing to me that she had been sexually abused by a family member years ago. At this point, my life changed forever; that day rocked my world. I suffered an emotional breakdown and just wanted to "stop." I didn't want to die; I just wanted to "stop" and not do anything. I wanted to be still and not go through the motions of life as if nothing had happened. I couldn't work for about nine months and was put on several antidepressants and became "zombie-like." Just walking and breathing, but not existing. I didn't want to "do" anything. I didn't want to function; I just wanted to be "still."

It also made me realize there is collateral damage. I realized my wilderness experience was rife with self-doubt, low self-esteem, and fear. I felt that I was a "weak" person that allowed this to happen to me. I remember during one of my counseling sessions, I made a comment to the psychologist that I felt I was "weak" because I wasn't strong enough to protect myself and speak up against the abuse. His response was, no, on the contrary, you were very strong because there are people that wouldn't be able to handle what you endured. He went on to say that what you told me and what I witnessed from your soon-to-be ex-husband during a counseling session, he couldn't fathom how I stayed in that situation for 24 years. He also encouraged me and said that I had to be strong to endure the harshness and the trauma. I realized that although my destiny was derailed by a decision, I still had not failed. You are not a failure of your mistakes or misinformed decisions. When you learn that you can move on to succeed and receive the blessings that God has for you.

It's very important to know that healing can and will take place over a period of time. The process of healing should not be rushed; you need to take that time to devote to "self-care" and get the support you need to recover. Please be kind to yourself and don't rush your healing. It is a process. It's also important to remember, that you can't allow the toxicity of others to poison you.

You are NOT "damaged goods." Your life is precious and should be handled with care and prayer. I have a sign in my home that states: "Life is Fragile, Handle with Prayer." Damage can be repaired. There is beauty in your "brokenness." The Japanese have a technique called Kintsugi that takes broken pieces of pottery, which they glue together with a gold sealant to repair them. Kintsugi is the art of putting broken pottery pieces back together with gold — built on the idea that by embracing flaws and imperfections, you can create an even stronger, more beautiful piece of art. These once-broken pieces become beautiful pieces of art. You are a masterpiece in the making. You are a diamond in the rough. You have gone through the refining fire and come out as pure gold.

You will continue experiencing the same types of setbacks, challenges, and failures... the same emptiness, disappointments, and fears... until you learn to believe that you are deserving of the things you desire.

You are not your parents. You are not the opinions people have of you. You are not your reputation. You are not your mistakes or your pain. You are more than the fragmented identity you've pieced together out of everyone else's voices replaying in your head.

You are greatness. You are a warrior. You are a survivor. You are everything you decide in this moment, made whole by the healing that you welcome when you refuse to agree with the idea's others have about the essence of what makes you, you... and that is where you find your power Within.

- o Do you ever wonder, why you're here? What's your purpose, what's God's plan for your life? I never really felt like I belonged anywhere until I realized my purpose.
- o When I asked God, why me and surprisingly, he showed me. I also realized that my decision had a "Domino" effect because others were blessed by their associations that led to marriage, children, and the creation of ministries.

I remember the moment I became liberated from the stronghold of this abusive oppression. It was the 4th of July weekend of 2004. I felt like I was reborn. I felt like I was 21 again. Freedom felt good. No more 911 calls, no more being the "laughingstock" of the neighborhood for the constant police visits. No more fights to break up between my spouse and my then-teenaged sons. No more damage to walls, broken doors, or broken glass.

> Myles Monroe said, *"If you want to know your purpose, ask the manufacturer." In other words, ask God. If you don't know your purpose, abuse is inevitable."*

That statement not only shocked me but helped me realize how important it is to understand my purpose. **Understanding your purpose will help you understand what you cannot accept. It is also setting boundaries of what you will and will not accept.**

The Cambridge Dictionary definition of abuse:

The use of something in a way that is harmful or morally wrong: *An abuse (= wrong use) of privilege/power/someone's kindness*

Cruel, violent, or unfair treatment of someone:
She claimed to have been a victim of child abuse.
sexual/physical/mental abuse (= bad treatment)

rude and offensive words said to another person:
He had apparently experienced a lot of verbal abuse from his co-workers.
He hurled (a stream/torrent of) abuse at her (= he said a lot of rude and offensive things to her).
"Idiot!" is a term of abuse (= an insulting expression).

In the excerpts of a book that I'm reading, ***"Learning to Be: Finding Your Center After the Bottom Falls Out"*** by Juanita Campbell Rasmus and Tina Knowles, the author shared an acronym from her therapist: DENIAL: I **D**IDN'T **E**VEN K**N**OW **I** W**A**S **L**YING.

This acronym had significance for me because, for many years, I was in "Denial." I thought that because there were no physical scars, I really wasn't being abused. This was denial in every way because I felt "bruised" inside. Eventually, those bruises became scars.

Non-physical violence is just as damaging as physical. Also, non-physical abuse can, in some cases, turn to physical violence. It's even more damaging when witnessed by children. What I have learned, ***children in crisis become adults in crisis.*** It is important to protect your children. Children become products of the environment that you have accepted. When you allow yourself to accept unacceptable behavior, you're unknowingly teaching them it's okay to be abused or to abuse others. When you experience abuse, seek help to understand what it is right away, and do not hesitate to get help.

One of my sons talked about the day of my breakdown after receiving devastating news from my daughter. He told the story of my breakdown and how it affected him. "Kick in the Armor" is a metaphor he kept using. I remember experiencing unbearable pain; it wasn't comparable to anything I could bare. He wanted to make sure I was okay when this event occurred, and mentioned that he couldn't talk to his dad, because he was devastated by what happened to me after his brother's arrest, and his grandfather's death. He reminded me about the time I attempted to leave his dad when they were very young. Unfortunately, I made the mistake of going back. I remember he voiced his disappointment that "we would miss out on a 'normal' life." In my children's eyes, it was back to bondage and control. In my eyes, it was back to the torture, the pain, and the never-ending battle of demonic oppression. I remember thinking, "What more is there to do? Please, Lord, help my children!"

There were moments when my children would learn nuggets of wisdom from their grandfather (my dad) and my now deceased brother. I felt that my family was lost, but at what cost?

At that pivotal moment, my son declared going forward "he would raise himself." He shared with me many painful memories that he endured that deeply hurt him.

Although the internal scars are still there, it's only a reminder of what God has delivered me from. I continue to go through the healing process. The difference between a scab and a scar – a scab means it's still healing, but a scar shows you're healed. A scar is a testimony. I'm still

evolving, getting better every day with new insights, a new way of thinking, and a new outlook on what's good for me.
Proverbs 24:16 ESV – For the Righteous falls seven times and rises again, but the wicked stumble in times of calamity.

Galatians 6:17 NLT – From now on, don't let anyone trouble me with these things. For I bear on my body the scars that show I belong to Jesus.

For years I wallowed in self-pity, asking the simple question, why me? Singer Deborah Cox put out a song a several years ago with the lyrics, "How did I get here? I'm not supposed to be here." Those lyrics spoke to me; I wondered for many years, "How did I get here?"

Then one day, after my "decades-long" journey, I realized that I was chosen to share my testimony to help others propel to their own destiny and purpose.

I didn't understand brokenness until I was broken.

When I understood brokenness, I realized it doesn't mean "damaged", I can now tell others that out of your brokenness, you can be mended.

I remember having a Women's Day program at my church, and I invited one of my friends to speak. The theme was "Lord Mend This Broken Vessel." What others didn't know was that the broken vessel was me. I suffered in silence for many years and wore a "mask" to hide my pain. My brokenness was a way of life for me; my vessel was empty. There was no oil left, no anointing left.

It's time to unmask your fears brought on by years of stress, tragedy, and loss. It's ironic that this pandemic has required the physical mask, although many of us have worn an invisible mask for years.

Stop accepting the blame for the actions of others. You can't clean up milk somebody else spilled. Blaming doesn't resolve problems.

Accepting the mistreatment and neglect from others can put you in a bondage of self-doubt, worry, depression and low self-worth. You second guess yourself by thinking that "maybe I don't know" what I need or what I deserve. The first thing I learned was that you should never allow someone else to tell you who you are and what you should be thinking or doing. When you realize the control of manipulation, you can circumvent it by understanding who you are and what you will and will not accept. Many of us are pulled into the school of what "other's think" we should or should not do. I remember being asked when I went through my separation and ultimate divorce, "If I was sure I knew what I was doing." Now remember, I was told that you should NOT talk about what's going on in your home or what you're going through because it's dishonoring your home. However, what I realized is that by not speaking up, you are not only dishonoring yourself, but also God. I realized that God did not create me to be misused, mistreated, or abused. He also wanted me to think for myself and realize that I had a mind that could not be controlled or manipulated. I realized that mistreatment is not "deserved," nor should it be tolerated. When God created Eve, Adam was not given instruction to treat her as if she was beneath him. However, when he looked on her, he was satisfied by what he saw. Eve was presented to Adam as a gift, as a supporter, as a help mate.

    I was asked by someone if I knew the "Will of God" for my life. As I began to think about the question, I realized that when God created me, I was "fearfully and wonderfully" made and was a symbol of his love through his creation. God never intended for any of his creations to be misused or mistreated through abuse. It is his will that all men (and women) be saved and not perish. He is a God of love and not damnation. He does give us free will to make a choice.

As I went through those very difficult experiences, I always felt like I didn't have a choice. What I didn't realize was that I had a choice all along. I had to choose to change myself and not focus on how others needed to change. God provided his word to comfort us, to guide us and to lift us out of situations that are harmful. Abuse or neglect that has not been resolved, is not how God wants us to live. Unfortunately, many of those that identify as believers would always say to others going through the storm to "just believe" and everything will work out. There is more to just believing you will come out of the storm of abuse; you must do something and not wait for something to just happen without doing the work. Unless the abuser is repentant for their actions and will allow God to heal them for true deliverance, those affected will always be under the bondage of those attacks. Romans 12:2 states: "Do not be conformed to this world, but be transformed by the renewal of your mind, that by testing you may discern what is the will of God, what is good and acceptable and perfect."

I realized it was abuse when I always shut down because of the intimidation. I was very shy and timid as a child and into adulthood. I realized that "timid" is the root of "intimidation." I was a target because of my low self-esteem and timid behavior, which unfortunately caused me to allow control over my life by others that took advantage of it. I didn't realize what it was until I began to question "who I was." I also realized there are "spiritual predators" who impose their so-called "prophecies" that only benefit them and are a weapon of control. I wrote this poem to articulate what my life was like:

Who Am I

I'm a friend without a friend.

A wife that never had a husband.

A mother that had children without respect. I have no purpose other than to serve others or connect them to their purposes. My help is misconstrued, and my advice is unappreciated.

Why Am I here.

No bonding, only bondage to the dream that never was or could be.

A life to serve only regrets for the moments, the time that was wasted on serving those that didn't cherish me. To serve a lifeless dream of lifelong regrets.

Running from an invisible bondage that is elastic and only pulls me back into the conundrum of pain.

Pain is life because I feel it. Life is not what it seems, but only deferred dreams make the heart sick and want to believe that this life was not meant to be.

I remember having a conversation with my oldest son (now an adult), who was battling an opioid addiction, he was very sick, and I felt very helpless. His erratic behavior and attitude are a direct result of the trauma he suffered from childhood, and I kept getting caught in the middle of it. I love my son and continue to pray for him; I had to get out of the blame game a long time ago because I realized it was destructive. I also had to realize I needed help because I was just as much a victim as my children. Fortunately, he was able to get the treatment he needed and has totally turned his life around.

One important thing to note, when you allow your children to witness abusive behavior, you are putting them in a situation they didn't ask for and systematically putting them in "crisis" mode. I said during a radio interview, "Children in Crisis become adults in Crisis." I capitalized on Crisis for a reason; because it will monopolize your time and cause you to be smothered in the web of abuse.

Frederick Douglass, an important figure in Black History, stated "It is easier to build strong children than to repair broken men."

CHAPTER III: MY AWAKENING, MY RECOVERY

I recommend three things to move forward and change your situation:

1. *Get up – pull yourself up by realizing there is a problem. By getting up, you're looking up. If you're in a physically violent situation, this is critical. You really don't have time to lose, especially if children are involved.*

2. *Get Out – seek refuge at a shelter or with family and friends that you trust. If you don't know anyone or any place you can go for safety, call 211 to get a list of the shelters.*

3. *Get Help – this is in the form of therapy through counseling, support groups, assistance from the spiritual community, and most importantly, trusted family and friends.*

You must realize that nothing will change WITHOUT YOU making the change. If you continue to live with the abuser, they WILL NOT CHANGE because they don't see the need to be accountable.

While I was going on one of my daily walks, the Lord very clearly spoke these words to me: "Don't be in debt to regrets. Don't be indebted to something that you don't have to continue to pay for."

Don't allow past regrets to put you in unnecessary debt; if past mistakes are lessons learned, then you've earned what you thought you lost. Learn and grow; past failures are growth opportunities. Nothing worse than the pain of past regrets. Rest because your best life is yet to come.

The Lord also encouraged me and let me know that "Although your destiny may have been derailed, you have not failed."

You have overcome when the hurt you suffered no longer consumes or controls you. You put it in perspective. To keep blaming yourself will not heal you from your brokenness. Use that brokenness to spring forward into your destiny and that pain to propel you into your purpose.

First and foremost, when you realize you have done all you can do, "Stand" and then get moving. Realize God has given you the tools to change your life, He will equip you with the courage and knowledge to move forward. The change must first begin with you by understanding you can't pray away something that you didn't cause; understand that God wouldn't want you to be in harm's way and especially if children are involved.

The second area you must focus on is planning. How will you leave and where will you go. Secure a location where you will be safe. Pack only what you and your children will need and if you have the means, only move the furniture that you will need when it is safe to do so. My awakening began, when I realized I had the courage and the strength to move myself physically out of the situation. One night when I was at work, the Lord spoke to me and instructed me to go to an apartment complex in the morning to secure an apartment. Then I began the process of gathering only what I would take and nothing more by securing a moving truck. Once we moved, I took some time off and visited friends in a nearby city.

Thirdly, God will give you time to heal. It will take time. You don't have to rush the process of healing. Selfcare is important and necessary. It's important that you don't stay stuck. When you're in the process of healing, the enemy will always appear to attach to you in your vulnerability. The enemy will try to mesmerize you and end up depleting you. It will try to suck the life out of you, and your destiny. Be conscious that when you make positive steps to change your life, there will be individuals that will try to latch onto you to suck your destiny out of you. Please remember that anything or anybody that tries to circumvent or derail your destiny is demonic.

As you heal, you will see that life can be good; take the time to savor the moments. There is positivity in desperation. When you're desperate enough, you will change and grow. Your desperation can lead to your restoration. You must have the courage to become desperate. When there's no remorse from the abuser, there's no recourse for recovery. What the enemy tries to block, God will unlock. Recite this affirmation: Because of God, we beat the odds.

What I learned about Healthy Relationships:

- *Disagreements aren't used to tear you down emotionally.*
- *You should never be put on the "spot" or second guessed because you have an opinion or feel a certain way about something.*

- *They don't compare you with anybody else or allow you to feel you're "not good enough."*
- *Do not use money, vacations, purchases, etc." as leverage to get what they want.*
- *Do not punish the other partner by changing plans because "you did something wrong;" therefore, "I changed my mind" about the trip.*
- *Do not isolate yourself from family and friends.*
- *Don't embarrass yourself around family and friends.*

Make the decision to break the cycle and seek help while you can before it's too late. It will get better. Seek support to heal and be kind to yourself. Understand why you were caught up in a situation that could have cost your life.

Understand that the simple act of abuse is a form of disrespect that simply crosses boundaries that should never be crossed. When you understand your boundaries, you will understand that it is an act of respect.

It is not my job to:

- *Heal others!*
- *Please others at my expense.*
- *Make it work if the effort isn't mutual.*
- *Continuously compromise.*
- *Tip toe around you.*
- *Anticipate your needs.*
- *Change myself to your liking.*

It is my job to:
- *Heal myself.*
- *Listen to my needs and my desires.*
- *Respect myself and my time.*
- *Be my true authentic self.*
- *Set healthy boundaries that protect my energy.*
- *Leave when I'm in danger.*
- *Say "No" when it's not in alignment with my values and God's word.*
- *Be mindful with my "Yes."*

The Journey to Resilience

The American Psychological Association defines resilience as:

> "The process and outcome of successfully adapting to difficult or challenging life experiences,

especially through mental, emotional, and behavioral flexibility and adjustment to external and internal demands."

I refer to resilience as a journey, because as you travel through your change, you will realize just how strong you really are. I learned that overcoming life challenges displays a strength that you don't realize you have, until you go through it. The process of overcoming is a component of resilience. To overcome is the first step to resolve what you must change within yourself. Change happens within you.

Adapting and accepting change will allow you to weather the storm of adversity. It will equip you with a new set of eyes. You will see things differently and understand that you can make a positive change. There are several factors that contribute to how well people adapt to adversities, predominant among them:

- Seek counseling to understand who you are, which will allow you to be more effective in a positive way when engaging with others.
- Seek out social services that will facilitate your changing needs. Understand what resources are available, such as housing, childcare, employment, etc.
- This is key for your self-care – seek counseling, training, or a combination of both to build your confidence and create a healthy view of yourself.

Most of the time, when you have encountered difficulties in life, you are misunderstood by those around you. That's why it's very important to devote time to selfcare. Seek counseling from a trained therapist and engage in a supportive group at your church or other social organizations where you can trust and feel supported. It's never too late to make a change. These two scriptures gave me the courage to change my situation:

"Beloved, I wish above all things that thou mayest prosper and be in health, even as thy soul prospereth." III John 1:2 (KJV)

"Thy latter shall be greater than the former," Haggai 2:9 (KJV)

Your obedience is what God desires, and he will redeem the time you think you've lost. From as early as I remember, I never worried about getting older. It was as if God was comforting me by letting me know that my "latter would be greater than my former." That revelation gave me the strength to endure and eventually overcome that very stressful episode of my life. Let's never minimize what abuse is.

Declare the following to yourself (unknown author):

- I'm not crazy, I was abused.
- I'm not shy, I'm protecting myself.
- I'm not bitter, I'm speaking the truth.

- I'm not hanging onto the past, I've been damaged.
- I'm not delusional, I lived a nightmare.
- I'm not weak, I was trusting.

Merriam-Webster 2022 Word of the Year: Gaslighting

Psychological manipulation of a person, usually over an extended period, which causes the victim to question the validity of their own thoughts.

The "Domino" Affect: Revelation of "Why Me?"

For years I wallowed in self-pity, asking the simple question, why me?

"How did I get here; I'm not supposed to be here." Those lyrics spoke to me; I wondered for many years, "How did I get here."

Then one day after my decades-long- journey, I realized that I was chosen to bring others to their destinies and purpose. I also realized that God actually "chose me." The pain that propelled my purpose, also blessed others.

After realizing this through God's revelation to me, I began to rejoice! All was not lost! I was chosen to begin a journey that revealed my purpose for bringing others to their purpose! My decision still blesses others and in the long run blessed me as well. It built my character; it strengthened my resolve. I told my children, "You are royalty" because they were born with a purpose.

There was a "Domino Affect" although I went through the pain of a misguided decision, God still got the Glory! He began to show me that my decision blessed others when I realized that:

7 marriages that created 20+ children have been born.

Out of the 7 marriages, 3 ministries have been birthed.

Out of my brokenness my purpose was revealed; that was the encouragement that I needed directly from God! It was not for nothing! Out of my brokenness flowed this anointing to write, to encourage, and to seek more of God's grace. I became confident in the faith; my courage equipped me with the boldness that I realized my purpose and I wasn't afraid to share it. What I thought was "broken", was mended.

But as my life changed and I began to heal, the brokenness began to flow with the anointing, the oil of healing the wounds of others who are broken. There is beauty in the brokenness; there is a "Balm in Gilead." There is hope. The mask has been replaced with the glow of a smile. The smile of peace, of joy even in turmoil, of hope that as I move in my purpose, I realize my pain was meant for a purpose. My purpose is to bring hope to the hopeless and breathe life into dead situations.

Hope is my new home; it brings me joy when I sometimes feel despair. Because when I think of his goodness!

Cutting ties with people who hurt you isn't enough; you must also cut ties with the version of you who allowed that treatment to go on!

You must release to have an increase. Release the negative to receive the positive; when you receive the positive, that is your recovery.

Although Trauma made me stronger as I came out of it, I realized that is also began to wear me down. *"I realized my trauma made me traumatized. It made me weak, gave me sleepless nights and memory loss, it gave me feelings I've never wanted. I made myself stronger, by dragging myself out of a dark place and dealing with consequences that weren't my fault."* @ Warrior Giddiest Training -

RK @ rkkaaayou

Perception and Self-Worth

My perception of what's right or wrong isn't misinterpreted by what I've been through. It is fueled by a keen awareness or discernment based on experiences. My value isn't dependent on others' opinions. Self-worth is how you value yourself.

Michelle Obama: Nobody can make you feel bad if you feel good about yourself.

Self-worth is **the internal sense of being good enough and worthy of love and belonging from others**. Self-worth is often confused with self-esteem, which relies on external factors such as successes and achievements to define worth and can often be inconsistent, leading to someone struggling with feeling worthy.

From Hopeless to Hopeful – Activating my Faith

There was a time in my life when I was homeless and jobless. By this time, I had relocated my mom and brother after my father's death. I remember we had just attended the funeral of my late uncle back in Minnesota; however, I didn't know when or where we would live. When we traveled back to my newly adopted home state in the south, I remember sitting in the car right before a job interview, my youngest son was with me, and I uttered the words "It's going to get better!" I had no idea when or where the blessings would come from when I turned my eyes towards the sky and I said, "God I need a miracle today." It was literally at that moment; I received a phone call with a job offer and found a place to live that very same day. I realized then, that activating your faith is an action. You must put the work in to receive the blessings that God has for you. James 2:17 (KJV) Even so faith, if it hath not works, is dead, being alone.

Understanding Forgiveness

As you go through the process of overcoming trauma, you will understand how forgiveness is the key to your healing. To forgive is for you, not for the offender. It frees you from the bondage of the control. You become free and the pain begins to heal.

I had a recent experience in which my children's father became very ill. One of my sons asked me to facilitate bringing them together to support their father. I didn't have a single ill-word or lack of remorse because I had forgiven him many years ago. I was sorry that he had fallen ill and prayed for his recovery. The fact that I could facilitate this reunion with their father proved to me that I had overcome years ago any bitterness that would have kept me stuck in a web of unforgiveness. You must forgive to move on.

Freedom through forgiveness means you're not stuck; you have resolved any bitterness or even hatred you may had held onto. Forgiveness doesn't mean reconciliation; it means you've moved on. You understand that we all belong to God, and we must forgive, just as God forgives us.

Understanding God's Will

Sometimes you may feel alone in your feelings to stay positive, especially when it seems almost everyone around you is negative. What I discovered for my survival and as I began my journey for God's will for my life, remaining positive in a negative situation is key to your survival. Remain consistent with your convictions when your life changes. What I desire does not override God's will for my life. I understand that being obedient is what God wants out of us, and he will grant your desires and wants based on your obedience to him according to his will. Don't let a bad decision derail your destiny. Again, I penned this phrase: "Although you may have failed, your destiny has not been derailed." Our failures are steppingstones to success.

God's will for us is that we don't allow ourselves to be put into bondage under the mandate of man. What this means is that, as a child of God, you have a right to be treated with love, honor, and respect.

It's up to each one of us to search our own hearts and know what the mind of the God is, as stated in: Romans 8:27 (KJV): And he that searcheth the hearts knoweth what is the mind of the Spirit, because he maketh intercession for the saints according to the will of God.

Romans 8:28 (KJV): All things work together for the good to those that love the Lord and are called according to his purpose.

Ephesians 5:17 (ESV): Therefore, do not be foolish but understand what the will of the Lord is."

Hope and Healing

As my life changed and I began to heal, the brokenness began to flow with the anointing. The oil of this anointing can also heal the wounds of others who are broken. There is beauty in the brokenness; there is a "Balm in Gilead." There is hope. The mask has been replaced with the glow of a smile. The smile of peace, of joy even in turmoil, of hope that as I move in my purpose, I realize my pain was meant for a purpose. My purpose is to bring hope to the hopeless and breathe life into dead situations.

Hope is my new home. It brings me joy even when I sometimes feel despair. Because "when I think of his goodness!" Cutting ties with people who hurt you isn't enough; you must also cut ties with the version of you *who allowed that treatment to go on!*

"The secret of change is to focus all of your energy, not on fighting the old, but on building the new."

Millman, Dan (2000) 'Way of the Peaceful Warrior: A Book That Changes Lives'

Progress can be in "baby" steps; healing is a process. You have what you need in you to move forward. If you have children, please seek help right away. You owe it to them to show them what healthy relationships look like. You can do that by getting involved in their school or church activities. You must protect them because if not, they will suffer from severe trauma that will carry over to adulthood.

"Some people will never change until the pain of adversity is greater than the pain of change. Until you change your position, nothing will change. Many will never change their position until the pain of remaining the same becomes greater than the pain of changing." Bishop Dale Bronner

To get started, take the first step by realizing that you are not by yourself. However, the abuser will not get help as long as you're still living with them. You must remove yourself from the situation and show them that they must be accountable for their actions. I realize that every situation is not the same, however, remember you and your children's safety should be the priority. If the abuser realizes their behavior is unacceptable, that's the first step to being receptive to help. Realize that YOU matter! If you have children, think about what they are witnessing. The unacceptable behavior of abuse will have a negative impact on them and will shape their view of relationships. Instead, they must learn that relationships should be built on love and respect. They must understand that no one should be mistreated or neglected in the form of abuse.

"Sometimes the smallest step in the right direction ends up being the biggest step of your life. Tip toe if you must but take the step." TobyMac #SpeakLife

CHAPTER IV: MY PERSONAL JOURNAL

I started journaling during the pandemic, and I wrote everything from short phrases to long poems to express my experiences. The information in this chapter are excerpts of my own thoughts I documented in my personal journal. The journal is my journey. These are thoughts that God gave me as I reflected on my life. Stop wishing and start working. If you think it, ink it. Write it down. Habakkuk 2:2 instructs us: "And the LORD answered me, and said, "Write the vision, and make it plain upon tables, that he may run that readeth it." I found my greatest healing through journaling my thoughts and allowing the words to flow through my writing. This chapter focuses on some of my journaling. It also revealed to me what the Lord was communicating to me personally.

Disconnected

Sometimes I felt so disconnected, but what I realized is that I'm being redirected by God's will and destiny for my life. Your path is your path; your journey belongs to you. You are uniquely you! Take care of yourself!

The Struggle is Real

But I'm blessed because while I hear the sweet refrain of lyrics, I can wander in my thoughts of hope that the struggle is real, but I'm blessed.

I'm living each day hoping that a breakthrough is coming, only to find it's only for those that are chosen. The struggle is real; the pain is surreal. Am I the person I think I am, or only the one that opinions have created? But opinions aren't real, or are they?

Designated Survivor

Survival is designated to those who chose that this pandemic won't catch them because of our cocoon of safety, which we think is a mask and gloves or the vitamin D supplements they tell us we need. No hairdo or manicures to keep up the image; I'm a designated survivor because I'm in God's Image. I'm a designated survivor, saved by God's grace.

Is My Pain Not Credible?

My story hasn't changed; it still has chapters filled with pain.

With each chapter, it remains.

Why has my pain not been lifted?

It's like my happiness has been sifted by the swindling of this life.

Am I not credible because of my pain?

The pain of rejection, the pain of no protection.

The sorrow of pain is of what gain?

Will I drift away in the silos of pain and wither away?

My pain is credible, although the scars are indelible.

It's incredible to me how God still sees me.

You say there's a balm in Gilead, yet these wounds still run deep to my dread of the disbelief of wondering how I got here.

You know what people think of you by their response to you.

In pain yet delivered.

Because I feel yet delivered.

No Healing, No Restoration – Know Healing, Know Restoration

One evening, I was conversing with my oldest son about getting counseling; he began to make excuses and comparisons between himself and his older brother. As he talked, the anger kept riding up like a flame that couldn't be extinguished. As I listened to him talk, yet another angry outburst related to a situation in the past related to his dad's behavior. I wondered, when will there be healing? When will there be Restoration?

Unmasked?

This invisible mask I've worn to cover my pain has been removed. No more cover-ups, no more masquerades. Keeping it real to show how I feel. Tired of acting when it's just protracting. No more hiding behind the mask of "everything is fine" because anything else sounds like a whine. Prolonged pain is no gain; stop the masquerade and get to your happy truth.

Answered Prayer?

I asked God for answers to understand why I'm still wandering in the land of "why me?" The answered prayer is my protection from those life events that could have brought destruction, yet I still see remnants of unanswered grief.

What is answered prayer, you may ask? Is it everything I ever wanted or only what I needed to show the world that God answered prayer because he did it for me? Sometimes, it may be no answer, which is God's way of standing back and waiting for YOU to decide.

Pain

I'm a walking ball of pain to my disdain. Hoping for happiness is a constant in my mind, even though this pain has me blind. Blind to hope, only seeing the same. Pain means you feel; tears mean you hurt; compassion means you care.

Muted No More

I've always felt like I was systematically put on mute. My voice didn't count because my thoughts were my own and not meant to be heard. Intimidated and extracted, left alone to mute my thoughts as well as my tongue. Speech muted, the pain of holding everything within is too much to bear. I reached true freedom when I began to express myself in writing; now, my words aren't just on paper but verbally communicated as I journey through my healing.

Original Song: Your Grace

Only you, my God, can wipe away my tears.

Only you, my God, can wipe away my tears.

Because it is your grace that gave me the strength to run this race.

By your grace!

By your grace!

It's by your grace, your grace, your grace.

It's by Your grace.

Oh, oh, oh, oh, it's by your grace.

Oh, oh, oh, oh, it's by your grace.

Only you, my God, can wipe away my tears; only you, only you.

Choir: Only you, only you.

I can run this race because of your grace.

I can run this race because of your grace.

Only God can help me run this race.

Because of your grace, I can run this race.

Only you, my God!

Only you, my God!

I can run this race because of you!

FROM PAIN TO PEACE

PAIN: <u>P</u>UTTING <u>A</u>WAY <u>I</u>NWARD <u>N</u>EGATIVITY

    Peace during the chaos. Content amid crises.

    Peace, where are you? The chaos of pain continues.

    Peace, where are you? I thought I had escaped the destructive behaviors that had tried to obstruct my peace.

    Where is my PEACE?

    Where is my calm in the storm?

    Oh, the comfort of peace.

    Peace in the midst of the storm.

My comfort in the storm is my faith that God would cover me. When I hear of the distress my now adult children express, I ask myself, how long must I pay because of the collateral damage they've suffered? How long must I hear the pain in their voices and continue to try to encourage them that "life will get better." As they continue to remember the pain of their past, I hear the anger that consumes them. The anger of pain can't be explained when I couldn't soothe the tears of my nine-year-old son because of my inability to stand up to his father. It festers over the years and becomes an inward oppression. I realized that my prayers were the only relief I could provide.

What balm are you using?

Jesus is the balm and healing salve that will heal our woes and pain.

Hope lives in my heart, and I believe it in my mind.

The balm helps in the transition of life that will eliminate strife.

Negativity breeds problems.

Refocus, rejuvenate, and renew.

Prayer for my children

Bring them into the knowledge of your guidance and love.

Banish the painful memories of the past. Give them a heart of forgiveness and love for those that have wronged them.

Give them joy and raise their mood by showing them hope.

Order their steps to move toward you.

Bind and destroy the strongholds of the past and let them know today is present and the future is the anticipation of your blessings. Bind and cast out negative thoughts and conversations.

Let love be without dissimulation, abhor that which is evil, and let all my children cleave to that which is good.

Bind confusion and all generational curses that bring about division.

Protect them from all danger, seen and unseen.

Keep them from all harm and deliver them from the afflictions of the body, mind, and spirit. Bind anxiety and depression that puts them in oppression.

God's Love

God's love softens the blows of life's problems and cushions the discomfort.

Declare with me: Today, I choose faith over fear.

Fear has no part in my life!

I will not dwell on negative, discouraging thoughts.

I will not be moved by what I see but by what I know that God is in control!

I am a victor & not a victim!

I am a conqueror & not a casualty!

Be unleashed. Don't let your trust (in God) rust.

Can vs. Can't

Take the "t" out of can't and say you can. I can do all things through Christ, that strengthened me.

Mute out negativity.

Mute out toxicity.

The Currency of Time

Time is currency.

You can lose money and get it back, but time is gone forever.

Don't allow people in your life that are time wasters.

You will be spent, and your life will be empty.

Time is an investment of your life; why allow yourself to be attached to strife?

Don't let what looks good allow you to make a poor investment of your time.

The Shame of Blame

Shame is nothing but the enemy's game to blame. There is a way out of this madness. God has victors, not victims. You didn't mess up; you just got into a messed-up situation. A diamond in the rough is covered to protect it until it can be processed to show its beauty. It is a process of fire, rain, and abrasions. God has a way of surrounding our lives to protect them. You are the diamond that God protected, watered, and cleansed by the spirit to do what God has called you to do.

An Agent of Faith

I declared that I am an agent of Faith; I must walk it out and not talk it out.

You fight fear with Faith.

My faith is the substance of what I hope for and evidence of what's not seen by my natural eye but by my spiritual eye.

Though you may be in despair, God is still there.

Uncovered?

Let's uncover our fears or doubts and face them head-on.

When Adam and Eve ate the forbidden fruit, they realized they were uncovered. However, God didn't cast them out of the Garden.

They continued together and maintained what God had provided them. Just as we uncover our fears, God forgives us.

However, he wants us to face them to overcome them.

Perfect love casts out all fears; just as God forgives, we must look at each issue we face as teachable moments.

We have "uncovered" what makes us human. However, God didn't cancel our callings. We are a powerful force in the kingdom, and we will represent hope to those that have given up.

The enemy seeks to get us off track by taking our focus on what God has already shown us.

Now is the Time

Now is the time. God brings the NOW, but sometimes we're stuck on THEN.
God orchestrated the change. Sometimes life is like chess; you must strategically make changes. Sometimes God will make a shift when you look like you're going to drift. Just before you go into a drift, God will make a shift. God had to take us from then to now to bring you into this season. God has arranged the change, so don't think it's strange. God has done this so that you may regain everything.

A Better Version of Me

Through all the trials and triumphs, I've taken the lessons of life and created a better version of myself. I broke through the chains of negativity that enslaved me and used what God gave me. I told my friends once that I'm the new "me" on steroids, because I understood my purpose. Can you see I'm a better version of myself? When you understand your purpose, your new home has removed everything toxic and replaced it with the power of being the better me, the peaceful me, the resolved me. Although my heart was broken, my spirit wasn't. The better version of me took me by the hand and pulled me up to keep it moving and keep me growing.

It's amazing that with all the negative reinforcement, I've found the positive side of life. I pivoted the negativity and made it positive. And because of the positive, I can live the life I've always wanted.

Psalm 18:3 states that during disappointment, know that God is listening and hears your cries, and will comfort you. He will always hear you, whether you are happy, sad, heartbroken, or disappointed.

Brokenness to Breakthrough

Before you get a breakthrough, there is brokenness. Brokenness prepares you for a breakthrough. The key to your journey is the patience and wisdom you gain while getting to your breakthrough. It is a process. The acronym for WAIT is Wisdom Available in Timing. It's all about timing. God is the author of time. It is in God's timing that we will reach our breakthrough. When you realize the areas you are broken, then you can begin the healing process. The analogy I use is if you've ever cut your hand, you realize the wound, then you clean it, add an antibiotic to keep bacteria out, and then you add a dressing or bandage. When you are wounded, it's important that you remove yourself emotionally and sometimes physically from the people or places that produced the wounds. That allows the wound to heal, and over time, the scars will disappear. Your memory of how you got the wound will exist, but it will no longer hurt.

The Maytag slogan was "**Built strong to last long**." About 5 years ago, the company changed it to **"What's inside matters."** That slogan is even more appropriate. It's what's inside; it's the internal workings of your mind and your heart that keep you motivated when you allow God to heal you and give you the strength to endure. Last year someone prayed for me and said, "You were built to last, just like Maytag." I wondered what that meant and realized that I was built to endure trials, overcome obstacles, or just "keep it moving" despite the pain of neglect? In my sorrow, I always prayed for a better tomorrow. I Thank God I'm still here. Just like the anxious student in the classroom of life, I keep raising my hand as if to say, pick me, choose me; I want to participate. In some ways, I've always known who I am. There were times I've had to fight the good fight of faith to withstand the pain of the consequences of a bad decision. I would observe others being blessed, and I would ask God, am I next? I learned that I had to prepare myself for what God had prepared for me. Just as Jeremiah 29:11 states, God had a plan for me, "not to harm me," to receive the happiness that I've longed for. There is a blessing in waiting; ask God for the patience to endure. It is better to wait on the promises that God has for you than to settle for what you think is good for you. What I learned is that you must have a healthy view of yourself; in other words, know "who" you are and "whose" you are. I realized that because my self-esteem was so low, I focused on others who were broken or viewed as the "underdog." I felt that I needed to be with someone that was "like-minded." I realized that this was a trick of the enemy to keep me down and not realize that I was the "precious jewel" that God made. Never discount yourself to cheapen your worth. You are a masterpiece, a "one of a kind" original that God loves, and he wants the best for you.

Although I cried, I know I tried. Through the years, I have alleviated my fears. Sometime the past will try to haunt your present. The gift of forgiveness is my present, and I'm no longer a prisoner of the pain of my past.

Although it seems that life has passed me by, my future is in God's hand as he guides me through the process of healing. I realized that God has always been with me, and my pain became my purpose. The tests and trials contribute to my testimony.

It's important to understand when you are embarking on a new life, ask yourself, "Is there healing in it?" Are you just doing busy work to satisfy others? How are your choices contributing to your growth? During moments of despair, I wrote this poem:

I'm brokenhearted; I'm back where I started. What can I do? What can I do?

Hope is kicking within my belly, like a baby waiting to be born. Just like labor pains, it hurts, but you keep pushing until that baby of Hope is born. Once you're delivered, you forget about the pain. You see hope, you hold hope, and you nurture it, just like that baby. Just because somebody knows your history doesn't mean they know your story. A Love Healed Heart is a heart healed by love. The songwriter says, "When nothing else would help, Love Lifted Me." A scar is a wound that has healed. What's in our hearts can't be handled by everybody, so be careful who you give your heart to.

For every rejection, I know it's God's protection. When I can't see, I know that God has guided me. I'm in his arms and protected from harm. He loves me, and that, I can see.

The Journey from Hopeless to Hopeful

No shoulder to cry on, no pillow to comfort my aching heart. The tears of my nine-year-old son, forbidden to be a Boy Scout, became the bitterness of a broken man. I was frozen in fear, afraid to make a stand; I was a mother, reduced to a child.

Afraid to hope, hesitant to dream. I wonder why it's so difficult to escape the disabling mistakes of my past. I was afraid to articulate verbally that my wants and needs are hidden away in my heart as an unspoken request directly to God. You could say I have muted myself so the enemy cannot hear and, therefore, can't participate in the sabotage of my dreams. My dreams cannot be stolen; my vision cannot be blinded. God hears me as I speak from my heart.

Hope and Loss

I created these two acronyms for Hope and Loss:

    HOPE: <u>H</u>aving, <u>O</u>pportunities, <u>P</u>ositioned, For <u>E</u>xcellence

    LOSS: <u>L</u>eaving <u>O</u>bstacles of <u>S</u>elf-<u>S</u>abotage A sense of loss is what I feel, but at what cost?

    A Loss can be a blessing, so cherish it.

What is Love?

Love is not a bomb dropped on you without warning; it's a process that blooms like a beautiful flower that's nurtured with the waterfall of understanding what's truly in your heart based on what you discovered in the gift of the person in front of you. It is the "what" to your "why." Love does not dissipate like water vapor when issues come but strengthens with the storms. Love is sure.

It's not superficial; it's deep within your soul. It's what you know for certain is your safe harbor of life's blessings.

Love brings life, hope, and joy that no matter what, it will prevail. It cannot and will not fail when it's deep within your soul.

A Mother's Love is the closest thing you'll get to God's Love.

Distress?

Why am I in distress when God knows what's best? You are my way maker, my company keeper, whom shall, I fear. My faith is fearless because your love does not cease.

Are you fragile or agile?

Do you break under pressure or bend with the wind of ebbs and flows?

Lord helps me to bend with flexibility that will never be broken.

Lord, help me in my low self-esteem and my lack of confidence.

My weakness is made stronger with God's strength. His mercy and grace carry me through the valley and gives me the strength to climb mountains. God is my fortress and guards my heart.

Communication: What's Driving Yours

Communication is like a vehicle. What vehicle are you using? Is it a luxury automobile or an unreliable beater?

The quality of your communication is equivalent to the quality of your vehicle.
Communication drives you to success or drives you into the abyss. Your effectiveness is the fuel, just as gas is to a car. Your effectiveness can accelerate your progress or keep you at a standstill. Prayer is the guide to understanding how to communicate effectively and edify.

What is safe? Is it being challenged, or is it a haven of mediocrity to feel better?
Safe is an acronym for "Seek and Find Encouragement" or "Self-Actualized and Fully Edified."
Remember, moving forward is not looking over your shoulder. Dealing with the negative residue through your

children is like experiencing the pain repeatedly. Learn to let it go, and just know that God has it under control. Keep it moving, your future depends on it!

Impress to Impact?

I realized that in following my purpose, I asked myself the question, "Are you trying to be impressive or impactful?" To impress is limited and can fade away, but the impact will provide the change needed to stand the test and allow what God has promised you. The pandemic does not stop the promise!

Faith Without Works

Faith without works is dead, is what I read, so why let fear take me to a place of dread when I know your protection will cover me no matter what is said?

Faith over Fear is what I hear ringing in my ear. Is it because I know faith without works is dead, or is it that I know my faith is bigger than any fear? Because what I see is distressing me. Oh Lord, do you hear what's in my heart so clearly? I can't let this fear take over by what I hear. What I hear and see will never take away the Faith I know is near.

I was meditating on the words of a song that I wrote in my head:

> "You can't block my blessings if you try, God has my back, and I know that's a fact. You can't block my blessing if you try."

For the anointing to enter, toxic thinking must leave. Before ministry can begin, healing must take place.

I Praise God to just be "Me."

I Praise God for just being me. I'm comfortable with me. I understand me. But most importantly, God loves me and has my life in his hands.

Bystanders or Friends

When I shared my testimony of overcoming pain, the thought occurred to me when sharing with who I call "bystanders" which are those who sit in judgment as they listen.

You listened with disdain. When I overcame and talked about my purpose, I could hear crickets. There was no sound to my ear to encourage me that, yes, you are on the right track now. Are you a friend that's praying for me, or are you a bystander on the sidelines? Let's be real - a friend is someone to stick close, closer than a brother or sister; a bystander is just simply someone standing on the sidelines, maybe wishing you well or maybe not but basically just watching. That's not a friend. Can this breach be repaired?

I realized that a Friend as written in God's word, is one that "sticked closer than a brother." A friend rides the waves of the storms with you and doesn't judge your journey. A friend is with you when you're down and celebrates victories of overcoming with you.

The question is: Who do you have supporting you: Bystanders or Friends

Faith

There's no such thing as "Name it and claim it." If you want results, you must "do" something. Faith without works is dead. And it's all according to God's will. DON'T MAKE NEGATIVE DEPOSITS EXPECTING A POSITIVE RETURN.

Discernment vs Prophesy

Jesus never used his status as the son of God to intimidate. To intimidate is a Pharisee spirit. I decided to write about these terms because as I went through my journey of overcoming abuse, there were those that questioned my decisions. Please understand that no one understands or can know what you have been through or going through unless they have gone through it themselves. Please do not let those that say they mean well belittle you by communicating to you in a way that is intimidating and have you second guessing yourself. Jesus never condemned those he ministered to. He simply said either go and sin no more or instructed them to share the good news that he had himself shared with them.

Discernment

The noun **discernment** describes a wise way of judging between things or a particularly perceptive way of seeing things. If you can understand something that's somewhat hidden or obscure — if you figure out the motives or intentions of those that you connect with, for **example** — you're using **discernment**.

Prophecy

A **prophecy** is a message that is claimed by a prophet to have been communicated to them by God. Such messages typically involve inspiration, interpretation, or revelation of divine will concerning the prophet's social world and events to come (compare divine knowledge)

Healing

Healing doesn't just mean the pain never happened. It means the pain no longer controls you. A scar is a reminder that you were hurt, but you healed. Storms kill some, and storms wound others. We hurt, but we heal.

Our testimonies are not meant to be kept. How can you tell your brothers and sisters you understand when you haven't been there?

"I will speak of thy testimonies also before kings and will not be ashamed. Psalm 119:46"

Keep on going. Remain strong, remain vigilant, remain encouraged, and resilient.

God is healing your scars, your feelings of intimidation.

To bring others to Christ, you need to be able to understand their needs and not sit in judgement. It's intimidating to those that are looking to the church for love. Jesus was the true example; he met people at their needs and brought them through deliverance.

Don't get lost in symbolism, tradition, and the legalistic bondage that has held our people back for decades and has done nothing but oppress. The Bible is a book of love and should be used as such to minister. It should not be used as a weapon to beat down the oppressed, to beat down the hurting, and to beat down those that we perceive as sinful and lost. In showing forgiveness and humility we are being transparent and that yes, we are human. You may be afraid to show your transparency, for fear it's like living in a glass house. The fear of stones being hurled at you, will no longer be an issue because you know God will build a hedge of protection around you. When you speak the truth according to the word of God, there is liberty.

No man on this earth has the power to determine how you will spend eternity, nor do they have the right to determine your destiny. Strive to be forgiving, and healing will take place.

The Difference between Dysfunction and Disruption

A dysfunction is a byproduct of generational curses within families. A dysfunctional family is a family in which conflict, misbehavior, and often child neglect or abuse and sometimes even all the above occurs on a continuous and regular basis. Dysfunction is like an illness that becomes a way of life in families that can travel from one generation to the next. The dysfunction of a family is the brokenness that God can break and destroy to bring healing and deliverance.

A disruption is an event, such as the loss of a loved one, a job loss, broken relationships (i.e., divorce), etc. For example, a job loss disruption will be resolved when a new one is obtained. Disruptions through life events such as the loss of a family member or loss of a relationship can be healed over time with prayer and counseling.

In the book of Psalms, David said, "Create in me a clean heart and restore the right spirit within me. You can't heal from what you're not honest about.

No one understands the pain of not being heard. When you are not heard, it is very disrespectful. When you don't receive a response to your questions, your insights, or your issues, it is very troubling. Communication can be complicated, even more so when you don't have a respectful, active listener. You may ask, what does it mean? To be a respectful and active listener means that you care about what the other person is saying. There should be no assessments or judgements.

There are 3 reasons why you might not receive a response:

    The listener doesn't understand you.

    The listener doesn't respect you.

    The listener doesn't care about the topic.

Communication is like playing double Dutch. Listening and hearing are two different things. If you listen, you will learn. Listening is a skill. You may hear something, but not understand or care about what the other person saying. The only baggage you should have is a bag full of lessons from your past mistakes.

> "My silence was grooming me; God's grace was proving me. You said to be silent no more because there is a message that people are waiting for. You must have a purpose, be on purpose and with purpose. You must be authentic from the inside out."

Realize Your Vision

As you begin to heal, you realize that you must get back to your vision. Habakkuk 2:3: Write the Vision and make it plain.

To focus on your vision, you must be accountable. Be mindful of what your focus should be and disconnect from past soul ties that held your mind hostage. Unhealthy soul ties disconnect you from yourself and your future. Romans 12:6 states "Be ye transformed by the renewing of your mind." Transformation first takes place in your mind.

Grow through as you go through. Everyone can be a "master" of their own lives when you allow "the" Master (God) as your guide. God's direction is the right connection.

Validate instead of intimidate; you are empowered when you validate. Toxic people will intimidate you and not validate you. The root of intimidation is "timid." Be mindful of the events when you allow yourself to be intimidated. As you continue to grow, pray for those that have intimidated you. Jesus was the true example; he met people at their needs and brought them through deliverance.

Don't fret over regrets!

Never wallow in past regrets! If you do, you will soon be in debt to things that you need to forget. Just because your destiny has been derailed, you still have not failed!

Dred negative thoughts, they are for naught. Believe that you have a healthy view yourself, because you are made in the image of God. You are fearfully and wonderfully made. Rebuild your sense of worth and strive for a positive attitude when you realize who you are in God's kingdom. God through his son Jesus, will coach you to safety, to peace, to love and unspeakable joy.

Walking Wounded

When you have been abused, you become the walking wounded; you have internal bleeding. Your brokenness is hidden; your scars are internal.

You cannot be anything to anybody until you become everything to yourself.

You must move on if you want to be smarter, wiser, better.

You are not being selfish when you are being self-focused.

What you believe is what you attract.

Eliminate the words "try" and "if" and replace them with "when" and "do."

Philippians 4:13: **I can do all things through Christ that strengthens me!**

You must expel the inward pain. Do not suppress it. Find a good therapist that specializes in domestic abuse and trauma therapy (i.e., PTSD).

    The non-physical abuse is very deceiving and is like cancer that consumes you. It creeps up on you and takes over your life. You rationalize that you can survive it because you're not being physically harmed. In many ways, this is the worst abuse because it takes over your mind. You begin to believe your abuser. You become emotionally drained, and you begin to disappear.

When I started on my journey of healing, I realized that some people liked me better when I was quiet. But that's not my new reality. Speaking up to speak out against the pain without remorse is my recourse to peace against the chaotic monotony of my former life.

Afraid to Speak

Afraid to speak, nothing bad but fear he would be mad because I had a mind to say what needed to be said. Afraid to move, no peace, only grief, knowing that there would be no relief.

Muted no more. Being unmuted is intentional! Muting is silence and silence is unintentional acceptance of unacceptable behavior.

When you have overcome pain, it doesn't mean it disappeared. It means it no longer controls you. We hurt, but we heal.

Healing doesn't just mean the pain never happened. It means the pain no longer controls you. A scar is a reminder that you were hurt, but you healed.

The disbelief of wondering how I got here. Understand that who you are in God's eyes is all that matters. You know what people think of you by their response to you, however, it has no importance if it is used to discourage you or derail you from your purpose.

Answered Prayer?

I asked God for answers to understand why I'm still wandering in the land of "Why me"?

The answered prayer is my protection from those life events that could have brought destruction, yet I still see remnants of unanswered grief. What is answered prayer, you may ask? Is it everything I ever wanted or only what I needed to show the world that, yes, God answers prayer because He did it for me?

An unanswered prayer might be God standing back and waiting for you to decide. Ask yourself, are you trying to help people more than gain followers. Remain consistent with your convictions when your status changes.

Stop wishing and start working. If you think it, ink it. Write it down. We are not robots.

Pain

I'm a walking ball of pain to my disdain. Hoping for happiness is a constant in my mind, even though this pain has me blind. Blind to hope, only seeing the same.

Pain means you feel; tears mean you hurt; compassion means you care.

Quiet No More

I have always felt like I was systematically put on mute.

My voice didn't count because my thoughts were my own and not meant to be heard. Intimidated and extracted, left alone to mute my thoughts as well as my tongue.

Speech muted, the pain of holding everything within is too much to bear.

When will my life matter, good enough but not good enough?

This invisible mask I've worn to cover my pain has been removed.

I am unmasked, no more cover-ups, no more masquerade.

Keeping it real to show how I feel.

Tired of acting when it's just protracting.

No more hiding behind the mask of "everything is fine" because anything else sounds like a whine.

Prolonged pain is no gain; stop the masquerade and get to your happy truth.

I Got Through my Wilderness.

For years I wallowed in self-pity, asking the simple question, why me?

Singer Deborah Cox put out a song a few years ago with the lyrics, "How did I get here; I'm not supposed to be here." Those lyrics spoke to me; I wondered for many years, "How did I get here."

As I was praying, asking the question: Lord, do you hear me? What do you want me to do? I cry, and then I wonder why my continued sorrow. Will it be different tomorrow? Shattered dreams and broken promises, when will my story become the unbridled happiness I waited so long for? Happiness is like an elusive bird that keeps escaping me. The voices that Satan puts in your mind to oppress you are NOT of God.

Then one day after my decades-long journey, I realized that I was chosen to bring others to their destinies and purpose. I also realized that God "chose" me for this journey.

But as my life changed and I began to heal, the brokenness began to flow with the anointing. There is healing for others who are broken. There is beauty in the brokenness; there is a "Balm in Gilead." There is hope. The mask has been replaced with the glow of a smile. The smile of peace, of joy even in turmoil, of hope that as I move in my purpose, I realize my pain was meant for a purpose. My purpose is to bring hope to the hopeless and breathe life into dead situations.

Hope is my new home; it brings me joy when I sometimes feel despair. Because then I think of his goodness…!

Cutting ties with people who hurt you isn't enough; you must also cut ties with the version of you who allowed that treatment to go on!

EPILOGUE

There is no such thing as a fairy-tale ending. There is, however, a process that will lead you to inner peace, which is joy, and the happiness you achieve is up to you. No one can create happiness for you, that's your responsibility. Each step, no matter how small, contributes to your healing and propels you to your destiny. You can and will achieve peace of mind and the freedom to seek a life of boundless joy.

Although I have moved on with my life, I still deal with the lingering issues that my now adult children are going through. What's changed is that I no longer blame myself or carry the guilt because of "what I could have done." We are given choices to overcome trauma, or to become buried in it as it totally consumes you. The best thing I could do for my children was to show them that you can overcome, you can be healed, and you can move on. To overcome is to gain insight, wisdom and most importantly compassion to help others by sharing the good news that you can "Transcend from Trauma to Triumph" Getting Past the Pain to Forgive.

BIBLIOGRAPHY

Brown, Brene' (2015) 'Rising Strong: The Reckoning, The Rumble, The Revolution'

Monroe, Myles (2001) 'Understanding the Purpose and Power of Woman'

The Cambridge Dictionary: Definition of abuse

Rasmus, Juanita Campbell (2020), 'Learning to Be: Finding Your Center After the Bottom Falls Out'

Douglass, Frederick (year unknown), quote

The American Psychological Association
   Merriam-Webster 2022: Definition of Gaslighting

@ Warrior Goddess Training - RK @ rkkaaayou
   'Trauma Made Me Stronger'

Obama, Michelle (2018) 'Becoming'

Bronner, Bishop Dale C. (2022) – Word of Faith Family Worship Cathedral

Millman, Dan (2000) 'Way of the Peaceful Warrior: A Book That Changes Lives,' page 130.

TobyMac #SpeakLife

Cox, Deborah (1998) Album: One Wish: "Nobody's Supposed to be Here."

www.ingramcontent.com/pod-product-compliance
Lightning Source LLC
Chambersburg PA
CBHW060031180426
43196CB00044B/2368